I0100859

The Woulda Been Room
© 2026 Zach Weiss
Observant Pinecone Publishing
Austin, Texas, USA

All rights reserved.
ISBN: 979-8-218-91132-4

Observant Pinecone
Publishing

presents

The Woulda Been Room

A collection of

children's poetry
for adults

Poems by Zach Weiss

Illustrations by Ryan Revels

for my grandparents

Jean Rothman
David Weiss
천선희 (Sunhee Chun)
손우석원 (Sukwon Sonu)

and their inner children

The Woulda Been Room

where things almost happened

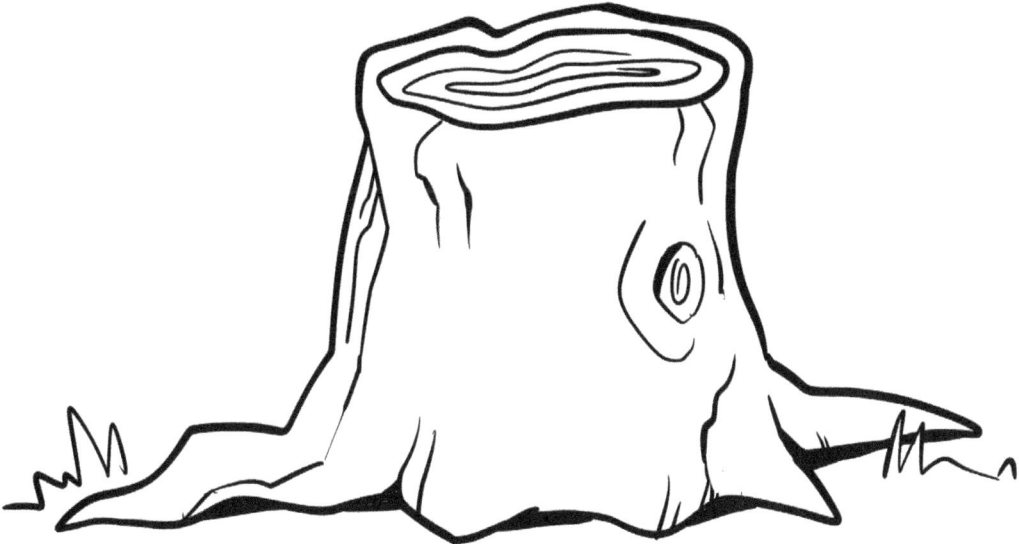

and almost will soon

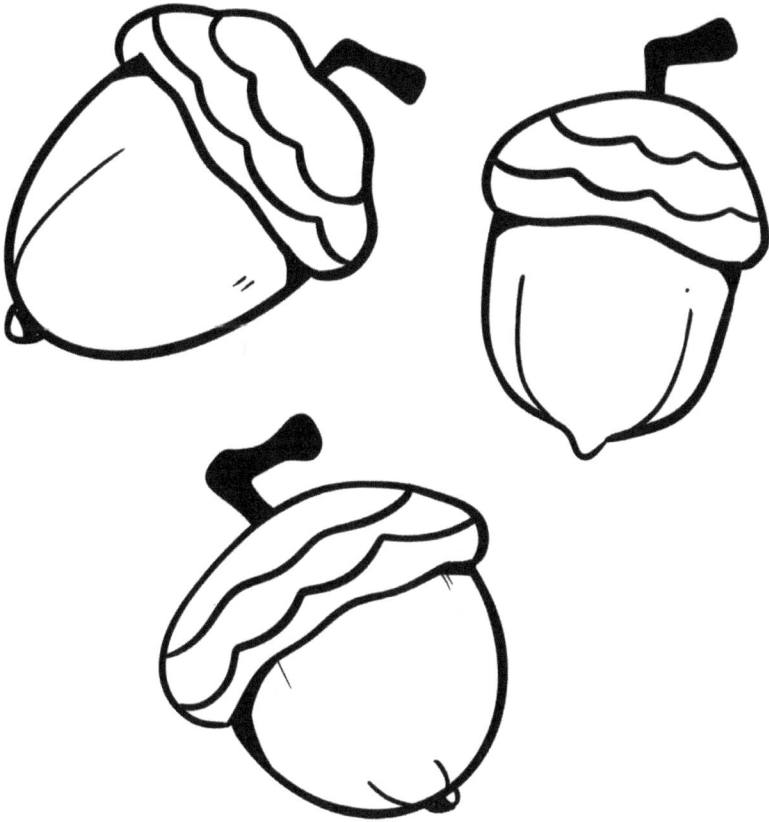

The Woulda Been Room

Welcome to the Woulda Been Room
where things almost happened
and almost will soon

Where things are bound to happen
at some soonish date
and will almost-er happen
the longer you wait

Where things are off by a fraction
missed it just by a hair
suspended in inaction
forever up in the air

Hear beautiful ballads and meet heroes unsung
answer phone calls unrung
mourn old souls who died young

Discover treasures unmapped
potential untapped
tempers unsnapped
lovesongs unscrapped

So stay for a while
put your feet up and chill
tell the Room what you're seeking
maybe find it you will

But be warned on arrival
if you stay for too long
that thing you've been seeking
may soon nearly be gone

At the end of the day,
it's up only to you
to step out of
or into
the Woulda Been Room

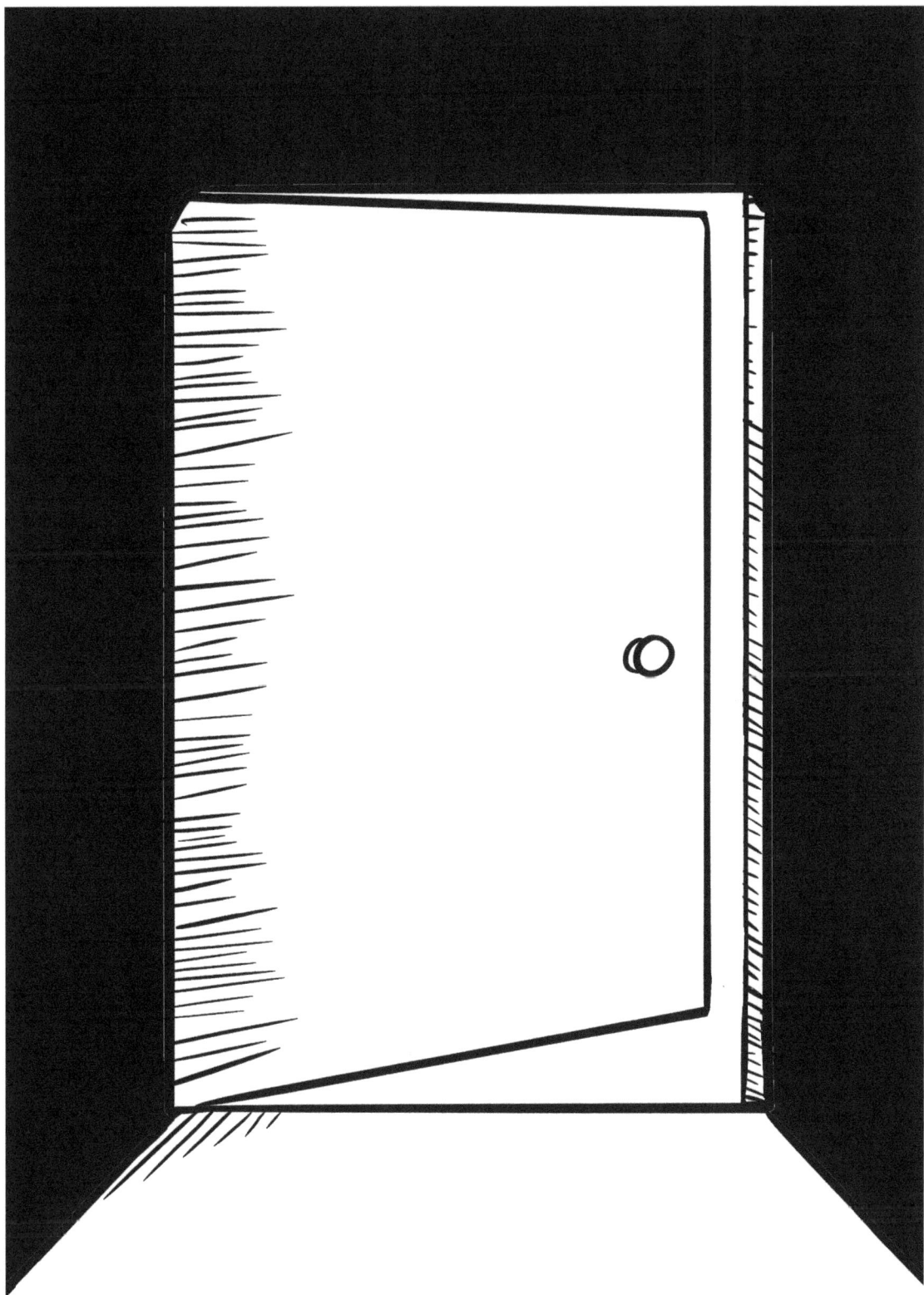

How Tall

How tall do I have to be
for someone to listen to me

Digging Mole

How did he get in this bottomless hole
He dug it all himself
He's always been but a digging mole
He knows not much of else

He's a hardworking mole
With an unswayable soul
Digging all day and all night
But the harder he shovels
The longer he tunnels
Further and further from the light

Will he ever dig out?
To him there's no doubt
But his friends have to wonder, from time to time
Would this hole feel so big
If he didn't just dig
And, at some point, he learned how to climb

But it's back to the grind
He's made up his mind
He's a mole, and his role is to dig

Prolific Writer

The Prolific Writer sits with criss-crossed arms
Away, apart from the rest
For a man overflowing with great ideas
What a strangely empty desk

He's a playwright and a poet
He writes epics just for fun
If you inquire about his memoir
He'll ask you back "which one?"

But hush! Let him write in peace
He's got a ton to do
Today alone he'll finish four novellas
Three shorts and two haikus

But the strangest thing about his works
They're still waiting to be read
The Prolific Writer's only problem
Is that they're written in his head

"I'll write them all down someday," he says
And he tries to now and then
"I'll be the greatest writer in the world
As soon as I find my pen."

Amir the Tear

There once was a Tear named Amir
Whose tale is still told around here
No matter how hard he tried
Amir couldn't be cried
So his friends always said he was weird

"Just do it," says Leer
A Tear from school last year
"What's keeping you here?
Leap out of the Eye, Amir, the coast is all clear"

Says Amir, "Hey there Leer, thank you for being here
It's true that I'm scared. I don't want to live in fear
I wish that I were different, and like all the other Tears
and could someday leave the Eye without dwelling on my fears"

Reminds Leer, "You know how it works, the life cycle of a Tear
No matter where you land, you'll end up right back here
It's not like you disappear, my good friend Amir
And once you're back here, you know that we'll all cheer"

Sighs Amir, "Hear hear. I know you're right Leer
I just don't know where I'll land, it's not exactly crystal clear
A Cheek? A Tissue? Who knows - it's all a new frontier"

"Relax," said Leer, "I don't mean to interfere"
Then he pointed to his own head and said, "Your fears are up here"
And then pointing to the heart, the heart of Amir,
"You have everything you need, right here, Amir"

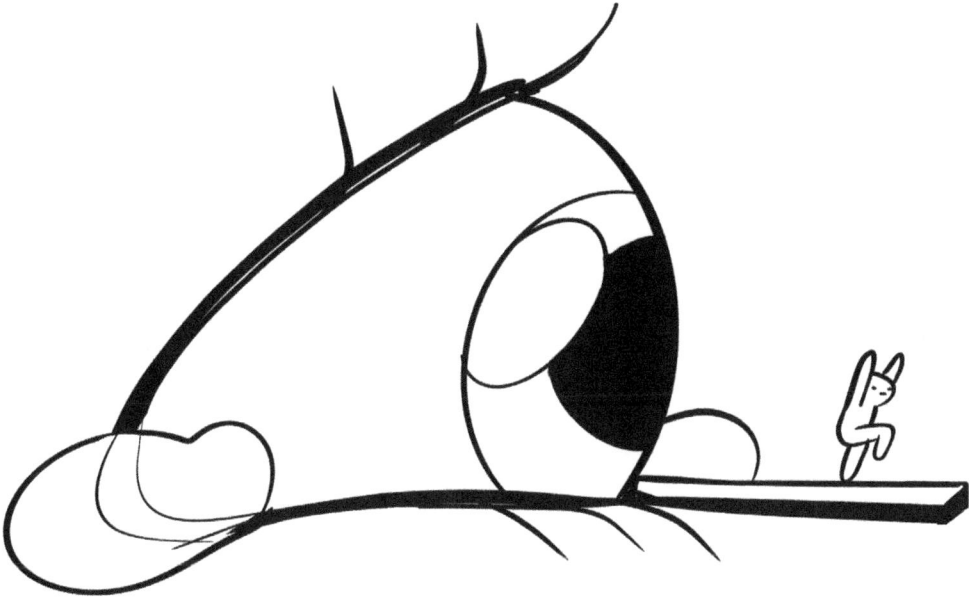

There was once a Tear named Amir
Who persevered and faced his greatest fear
At long last he tried
Amir leapt out of the Eye
And came back with stories and souvenirs…

And his tale is still told around here
The Tale of Amir, the Tear
in the Beard

Diva Rooster

"It's 6:42, Cockadoodledoo"
Sing the roosters from up on their roosts
A cacophony of sounds
Wattles moving up and down
But the fact is they're all out of tune

Could somebody teach these dudes to sing please
Their harmonies make me weak in the knees
Their timing makes me woozy
Their rhythm what a doozy
And they sing in a dozen different keys

But then the light shines bright, on little old me
And the time is right for the whole world to see
I'm the star of the show
So I wait, and I crow
"It's 6:43, Cockadeedledee"

Mountain Boat

I built a boat with my bare hands
to conquer my sailing fears
But I was so afraid of getting wet
I built it all the way up here

Thank You

Thank you for holding me
        when I thought I was unhuggable
Thank you for reaching out
        when I thought I was untouchable
Thank you for reminding me
        when I thought I was not enoughable
Thank you for warming me
        when I thought I was unnumbable
Thank you for pushing me
        when I thought I was unshovable
Thank you for pulling me
        when I thought I was untuggable
Thank you for cleaning me
        when I thought I was unbrushable
Thank you for calming me
        when I thought I was unhushable

Thank you for loving me
        when I thought I was unlovable

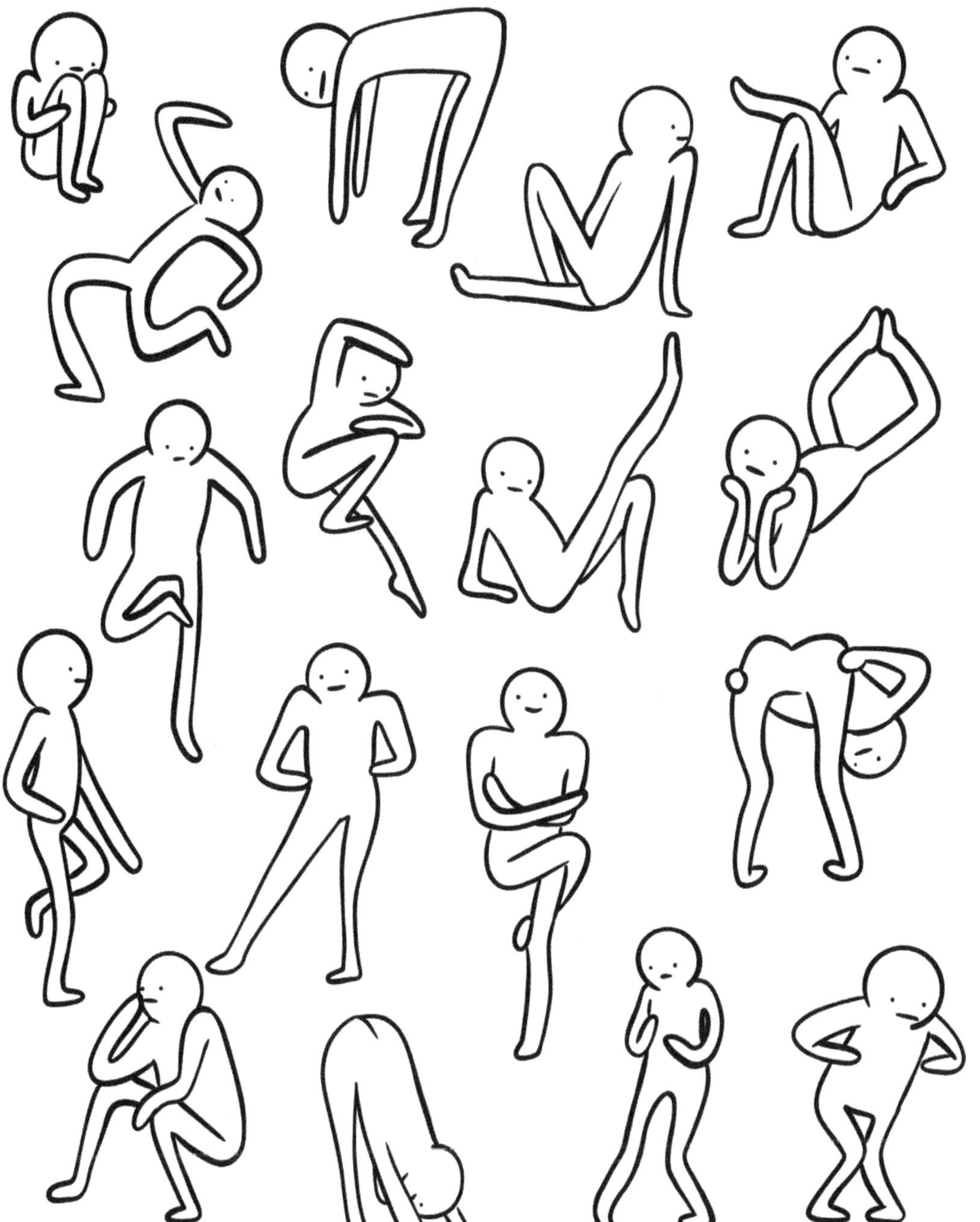

The Chameleon

Mirror mirror on the tree
which color today will I be

If green calls me, I'll pick up and be filled
inspired, determined, I can climb any hill

I can soak in sad blues
and embrace heavy truths
I can wallow in tired grays
I don't ever need to move

If it's time to be red I'll let the blood rise to my head
and make another foe or friend
I'll be quick, I'll be sharp
I can sleep when I'm dead

I can daydream in pink & in orange sunset skies
I can melt into amber, into the hazel of her eyes

I can be any color that I want to be
the only problem is what color is truly me?

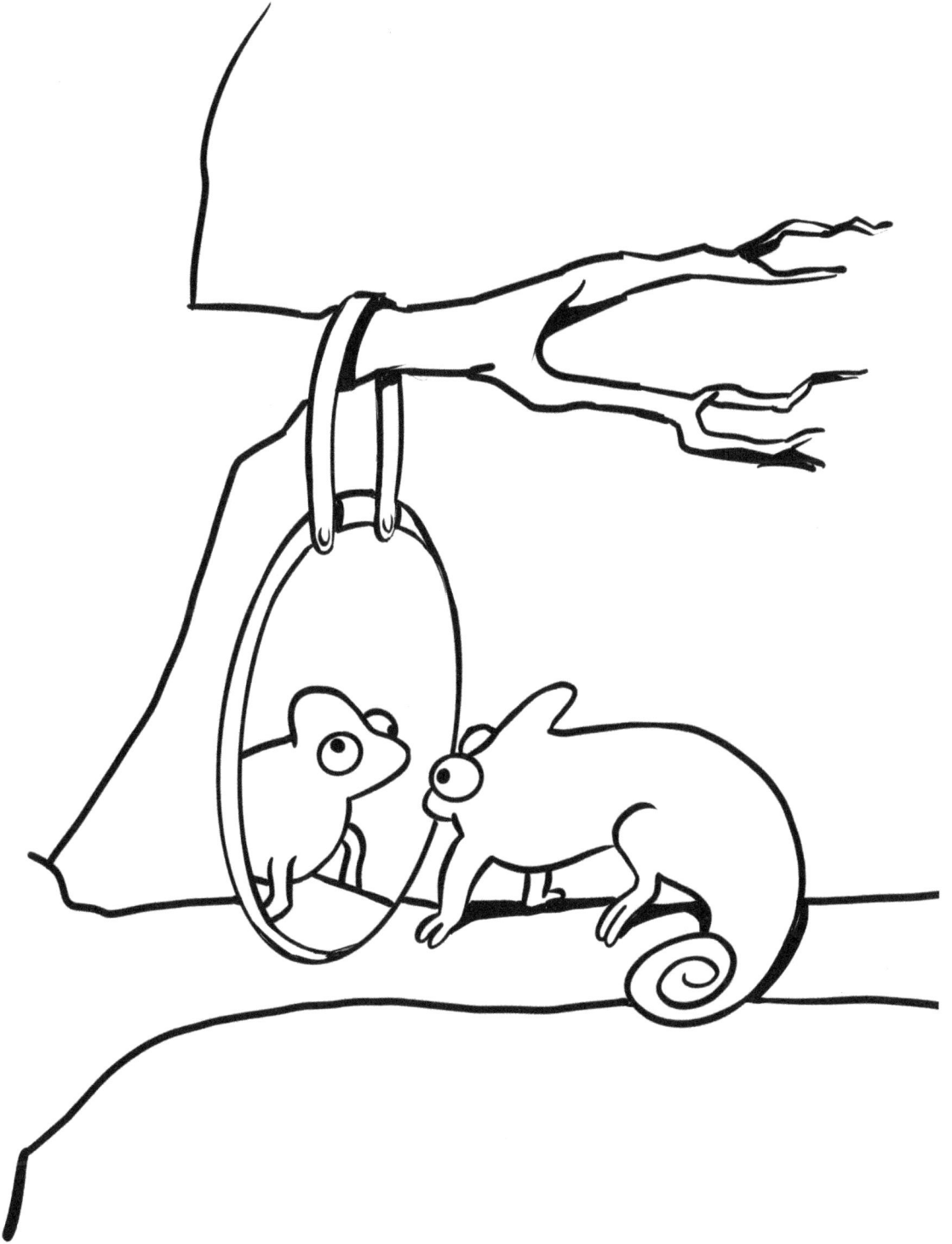

Come take a trip on my coffeeship

Come take a trip on my coffeeship
It runs on ideas and caffeine
We'll sip as we sail through the universe
Passing planets that we've never seen

Espresso for me as we pour over Uranus
Feeling frothy as we flip around Mars
No judgment as we jaunt over Jupiter
Sharing secrets out here under the stars

Could we lower the volume on that supernova
I want to hear what you have to say
What's your opinion on oat, soy, or almond
I like mine the real Milky Way

We'll sit and we'll chat
And we'll chit - look at that!
And the ship will sail on, past the moon

We'll stew, and we'll think
We'll brew, and we'll drink
Need sugar? Not a problem, pass the spoon

Our time, just a bang and a flash
Fill my cup, I want more than a splash
May we sip here together
May our trip last forever
And may we never, ever, have to

crash

Hooked

I'm caught on her hook
she's caught on mine
we lift each other up
all of the time

Hot Potato

Hot potato, hot potato
Burning in my hands
Your fire once felt so good
But now this pain I can't stand

I know your warmth, your love, your feel
Your spots, your shape, your grooves
It's hard for me to think of a world
Where my hands aren't holding you

My right hand will grow lonesome
And my left will be confused
And without you to have and hold
they won't know what to do

But hot potato, hot potato
I need to put you down
It'll be cold and painful for a while
Without your warmth around

But the cold will someday stop
The world will regain its color
And my hands won't be so empty
For now, they'll hold each other

Wait a minute...

Sick Beaver

Sick day, sick day
Weaver the Beaver needs a sick day
They'll say, they'll say
Does he really need a sick day?

"Hey there Mr. Beaver Boss,
I'm feeling kinda off today...
in my head, my heart, and my soul
You know how Beaver life can be
sometimes it takes a toll"

"Weaver, we've got a dam to build
We don't feel on company time.
Your insides quite unmatter here
As long as your body's working fine

After all...

Your teeth still chop
Your jaw still chews
Your fur feels fine
Your skin's unbruised

Your tail still pats
Your hands don't shake
Your legs don't wobble
Your feelings can wait!"

So Weaver went to work
And his body did have what it takes
It's just hard to build a dam
When a beaver's heart aches.

Four Leaf Clover

I found a four leaf clover
Today's my lucky day
My life's about to change
With all the luck that comes my way

This clover that I found
Is as special as can be
Instead of having four leaves
Mine has only three

Most clovers aren't shaped like mine
If you're surprised, then don't be
Instead of leaves that are dull and round
Mine are sharp and pointy

They say that if you want its luck
You have to rub it on your skin
So I rubbed it and rubbed it all over mine
So all the luck would rub on in

Now I'm scratchin', scratchin', scratchin'
Wishin', maybe I'd be
A little luckier next time around
And not Itchin' from Poison Ivy

Crystal Ball

I bought myself a crystal ball
But this whacky thing is broken
It's solving all my problems
Way less than I was hoping

Give it a try, stare into its glow
Think of your worstins' and your bestins'
No matter what you ask this ball
It comes askin' back the same question

Wait a second for it to think
Without fail it comes a'peeking
Swirling whirling in a cloud
"What are you really seeking?"

Used-to-Be Magician

Abra
Kadabra
Alaka.. Zee?
Oh, the magician that I used to be
But that was long ago
What happened to me

Abra
Kadabra
Alaka…Zong?
How did it go again
did I say the words wrong

Abra
Kadabra
Alaka…Zeer?
I used to be able
to make rabbits disappear
Could you spare me a nickel
It's here, behind your ear

Abra
Kadabra
Alaka…Zo?
What happened to the things
That I used to know
What happened to the way
That I used to glow
What happened to my magic
Where did it all go?

Bouncy Ball

Once there was a ball, bouncing in the middle of the hall
No one saw who threw it, we couldn't make the call
But soon a crowd had gathered to witness the ball
That bounced from wall to wall in the middle of the hall
And showed no signs of slowing down at all

And then an open door, from Classroom 1654
It's the mathematics teacher, Mr. Montague Maglore
Whose hippy hair hung down so low it almost touched the floor
"This ball, it moves so fast, unlike any I've seen before
What incredible velocity, every minute, it quadruples
Though if it keeps this pace, then I can't teach my pupils."

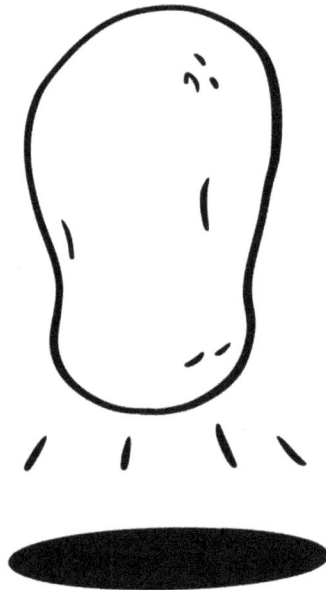

Here comes Mrs. Meeker, the history teacher,
Who yells in a voice that couldn't be screechier
"Stop bouncing that bouncy ball in the middle of the hall,
I'm trying to teach a lesson about Charles de Gaul
And I can't focus at all with balls bouncing on my wall

Maglore turns and yells, "Meeker you're not alone
You're not the only one to wish this ball were still as stone
How did this happen? I wish I could've known
To watch for who threw the ball in this hallway alone
But as you can see, this ball's been thrown
And that ball seems to have a mind of its own

Now at the scene is Coach Luis
Pucks, Bats, and Balls are his expertise
With big muscles bulging right out of his tee
If anyone can stop the ball, it'll surely be he
But Luis yells "Holy Crumb!" and he drops to his knees
"Never have I seen a ball bounce with such speed
Only a fool would be so unwise to impede
This ball on its path, with the force of a stampede."

Though Luis was no fool, he kept his wits cool
And knew in his heart, and by the unwritten rules
It was the P.E. teacher's job to keep track of his tools
That he must be the one to bring calm back to the school
And bring calm to the hall, and put a stop to the ball

Out stepped Coach Luis, with a chest of concrete
He stood tall strong and firm, and didn't try to retreat
Eyes closed and teeth clenched, ready to meet
The ball as it came and knocked him clean off his feet
And he fell to the floor, I had a front row seat
But after a moment he rose to his feet
And proved to the school he couldn't be beat
While the ball slowed and it slowed until the thing was complete
And it rolled to a standstill, the mark of defeat

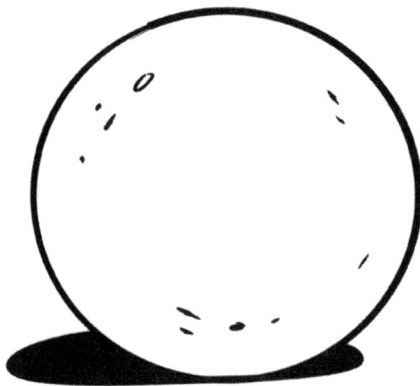

That was the day, the day when the ball
Bounced out of control all over the hall
It could've been bad, but Luis answered the call
A hero among us, we'll always recall
The day that he brought peace and quiet back to the hall
For once…but not for all…

Kids gone and halls empty where the commotion had been
So quiet you could hear the drop of a pen
I waited
and waited,
and that's when I then
came back in the hall
and I threw the ball
…again

Lost Homework

If I don't find my homework, I don't know what I'll do
I'll tell my teacher, "I swear I did it!" but she won't think that's true
And then she's gonna get so mad, she'll kick me out of school
And then I'll never learn the things I'll wish I always knew

If I don't find my homework, my friends will think I'm dumb
I won't be able to show my face, and I'll have to go on the run
I'll be on my own forever, and it won't be any fun
But that's the way it'll have to be, with my homework left undone

If I don't find my homework, I'll have a lousy job
Like cleaning portopotties or putting corn back on the cob
And late on lonely sleepless nights, I'll wonder and I'll sob
About how I came to be such a sad old lonesome blob

If I don't find my homework, I won't have any money
I'll go hungry on the streets with a wailing empty tummy
I'll never have a family, and no one will ever love me
That'll be my life, the life of an unloved dummy

If I don't find–
Oh wait, there it is

Scheming Fly

Someday one day
They'll finally see
The mistake they made
When they passed up on me

I'm awesome and attractive
And talented too
I'll blossom, and that's when
I'll come back into view

And watch all of them watch me
And feel all of their eyes
As I fly high, high, high
Up into the Sky

"There goes that Cool Fly
Up into the Sky
What was I thinking?
I can't believe I
Could have passed on the chance
To be nice to him then
I would do it so different
If I could do it again."

Someday one day
They'll finally find
That I was a cool fly
And was cool the whole time

Almost Right Calculator

My calculator is rather rare
The only one of its kind
He's always nearly almost right
One hundred percent of the time

For a while he'll be number-crunching along
Flawless, no need to fix
But then he gets all turned around
And turns a nine into a six

Point five rounds up, sometimes
And he'll never tell you when
His favorite number is ninety nine
Just one away from ninety ten

He says
"Numbers are such simple shapes
So unsophisticated
An extra zero never hurt and
precision's overrated
It's good enough to be almost right
It's not that complicated."
So I asked him what is 4 times 2
And I waited and I waited

And when he finally gave the answer
I returned him to the shop
This almost right calculator thinks
4 times 2 is 8 o'clock

Grandfather Clock

All these years
says the Grandfather Clock
and still so many questions
about what makes me tick

Quiet Garden

Shh–
Keep your body still
And your voice down to a whisper
The moment will last longer
And the air will feel crisper

The dandelions will tell you
Things you never knew
Like how to spend your time
When you don't know what to do

The breeze will compliment your skin
And ask your hair to dance
And you surely won't regret it
If you choose to take the chance

Be ready with the answer
When a rose asks you a riddle
Like what color does a tulip turn
When it bends over, down the middle

There's beauty all around you
You don't know what you're missin
Just sit back and take a breath
All you have to do is listen

Cool Hat

Everyone's gonna judge me
Everyone's gonna laugh
Everyone's gonna say
"Look at that awful hat!"

I know it's kinda different
I've never worn this style
Trying something different?
I haven't tried it in a while

I'm worried now - should I take it off?
Should I have saved it for a later date?
But I'm already here, there's people round
It's really much too late

Here comes Ericka
on her way to welcome me in
But as I worry what she'll say about my hat
She just says "Hey friend, how ya been?"

Across the room, I feel a stare
So I adjust my hat and fidget
But then I see a pair of friendly smiles
And I wave back to Wayne and Bridget

I bump into Brian
We talk about his cat
He said he likes my shoes
No mention of the hat

Whitney waxed poetic
About some rumors she denies
But I didn't mind the gossip

I had a great time at the party tonight
I felt good in my Cool Hat
No one said or did a thing about it
and that
right there
was that

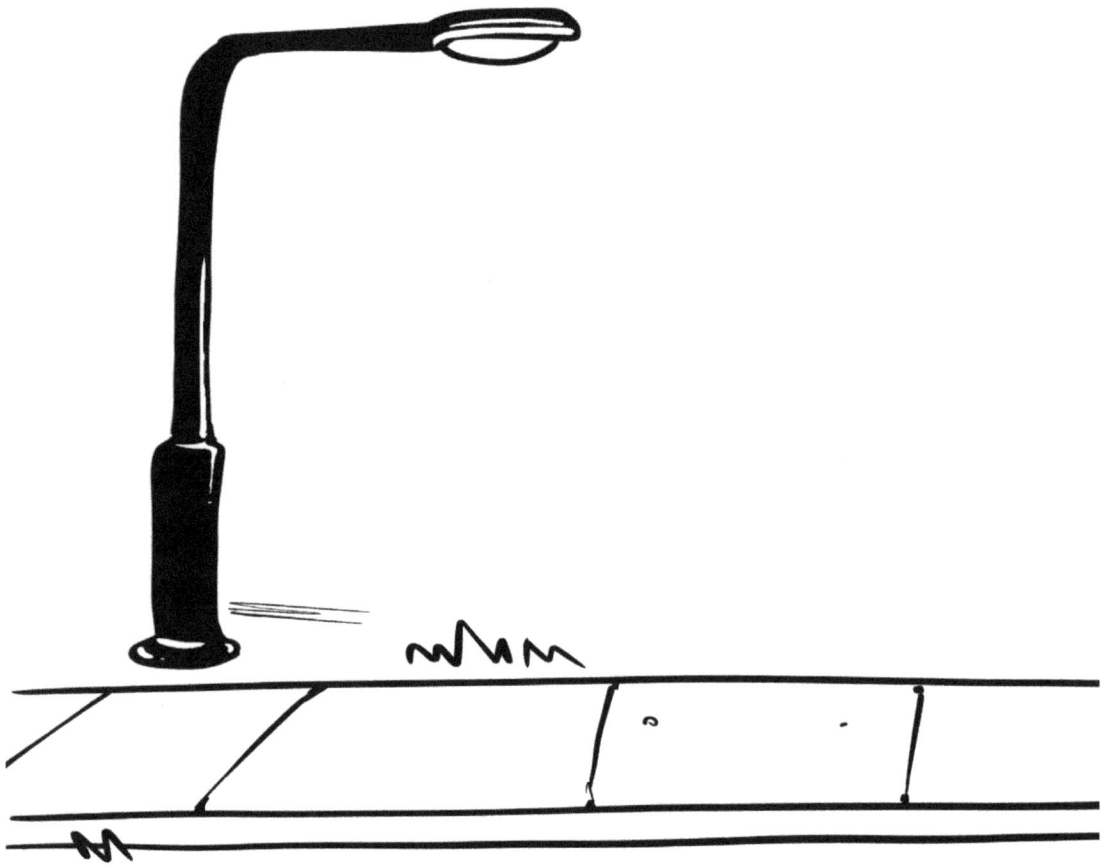

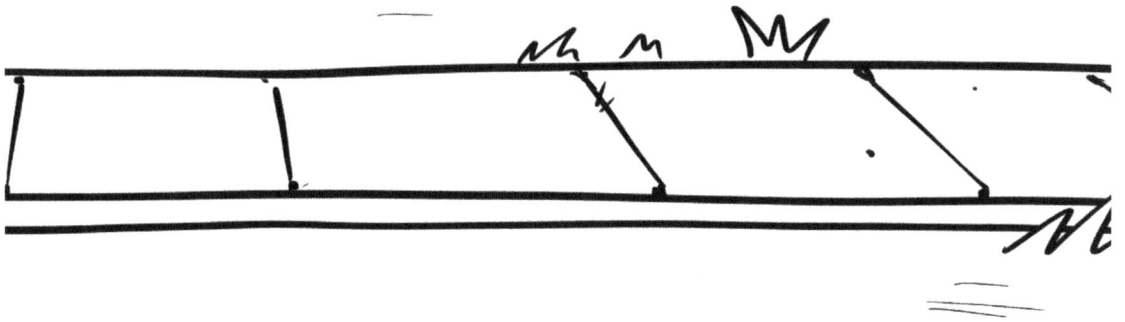

About Zach

Zach is an aspiring prolific writer, a data scientist by trade, and a men's group facilitator in his spare time. He is energized by long Saturday mornings, intimate conversations with strangers, and breakfast burritos with soft potatoes and crunchy bacon. He hails from Los Angeles and currently lives in Austin, Texas with his three dogs: Cora, Saja, and Kizu.

About Ryan

Ryan is an artist based in Austin, Texas who works from intuition, mood, and whatever is unfolding in her life at the moment. She spends her time drawing, journaling, and turning her thoughts into images that feel honest and expressive. She likes quiet mornings with her dog Bear, making things from scratch, and hangs with friends that last all night. Her work is emotional, direct, and always evolving.

Thank you for reading

The Woulda Been Room

www.ingramcontent.com/pod-product-compliance
Lightning Source LLC
Chambersburg PA
CBHW041601260326

41914CB00011B/1349